You have the greatest power and presence still active and available to you. His name is Jesus Christ.

I AM IS ALL

WE NEED

ROY ELTON BRACKINS
"THE CARDINAL"

Editing and typesetting: Inksnatcher.com
Cover design: German Creative
Cover photo: Kevin Carden

Ordering Information:
Quantity sales. Special discounts are available on quantity purchases by corporations, associations, and others. For details, contact the author through the website above.

I AM Is All We Need/ Dr Roy Elton Brackins —first ed.
ISBN 978-1721525614

This book is dedicated to Jesus Christ. He has proven Himself over and over again to be all that I truly need.

Contents

INTRODUCTION TO
I AM IS ALL WE NEED

THERE ARE MANY people dealing with
inadequacies and insufficiencies in their lives.
This group of people also includes many of us
who are a part of the body of Christ. In most
instances we feel inadequate and full of
insufficiencies because we have lost focus of
who we are connected to and who we should
remain committed to. We need to be
reminded that we serve an all-loving, all-
knowing, and all-sufficient God; yet we are
living as if we are dependent upon ourselves
for the meeting of our daily and eternal needs.

I am by no means suggesting we do not
have real needs in our lives, but the problem
could very well lie in the fact that we are
seeking satisfaction from the wrong, and
sometimes even ungodly, sources. Many

individuals are trying to fill those voids with more people, more possessions, or even a greater level of popularity. The discovery I have made is that we have become so distracted with what we feel we want, we have completely lost focus on *who* we really need in our lives.

When I consider the person of Jesus, the power of Jesus, the protection of Jesus, and the perpetual provisions of Jesus, one thing is abundantly clear. He has and He is the answer for all our dilemmas. He is the great I AM. I can say unapologetically, with boldness and authority, I AM is all we need! There are no ifs, ands, or buts about it. If we will focus more on pursuing His heart, we will discover He has everything we need in His hand. But I must issue a word of caution that will be repeated throughout this book. We will never receive what we desire from the hand of God until our number one priority becomes the pursuit of the heart of God.

In the Gospel of St. John, Jesus made seven premier and prominent statements about Himself. He never said, "I was"; He never said, "I will become." He said, "I AM." The I AM statements provide the foundation for this book. Let's dig in and strive to discover collectively the assurance in knowing that I AM is truly *all* we will ever need.

Dr Roy Elton Brackins
"The Cardinal"

I Am the Bread of Life

You seek Me, not because you saw the signs, but because you ate of the loaves and were filled. Do not labor for the food which perishes, but for the food which endures to everlasting life, which the Son of Man will give you, because God the Father has set His seal on Him."

Then they said to Him, "What shall we do, that we may work the works of God?"

Jesus answered and said to them, "This is the work of God, that you believe in Him whom He sent."

Therefore they said to Him, "What sign will You perform then, that we may see it and believe You? What work will You do? Our fathers ate the manna in the desert; as it is written, 'He gave them bread from heaven to eat.'"

Then Jesus said to them, "Most assuredly, I say to you, Moses did not give you the bread from heaven, but My Father gives you the true bread from heaven. For the bread of God is He who comes down from heaven and gives life to the world."

Then they said to Him, "Lord, give us this bread always."

And Jesus said to them, "I am the bread of life. He who comes to Me shall never hunger, and he who believes in Me shall never thirst.

— John 6:26–35

1

SATISFACTION
GUARANTEED

And Jesus said to them, "I AM *the bread of life."*
— *John 6:35, emphasis mine*

I WILL BE THE FIRST to admit I have a tremendous amount of hesitancy when it comes to new methodologies and trying new things. I tend to become adjusted to doing things a certain way, and I am taken out of my comfort zone when I am forced or challenged to do something that will call for a dramatic

1

change in my normal pattern and my regular routine. One of the reasons I feel this way is because in my mind, the way I am doing what I am doing seems to be working for me and providing me with the level of effectiveness I strive to attain.

There have been times when people have offered suggestions to me about making some adjustments, either by addition or deletion of something, that can either help or hinder my productivity. It is during these times when I ask both them and myself one main question: Is what you are recommending going to add to my ability to be more productive, or is this simply something you want me to try because this is the way you do it? Then I begin to examine the kind of commitment, effectiveness, and level of productivity present in the life of the person making the suggestion. My mindset is,

> *If your life is lacking in the areas of stability, excellence, and moral fortitude, then why should I take your advice if it is not even working to make you a better person?*

WHAT'S THE FRUIT?

I have shared this with you in the form of my introduction, because I believe these may have been some of the thoughts on the minds of the scribes, Pharisees, Sadducees, and other religious leaders during the earthly lifetime of Jesus Christ. I want to give them the benefit of the doubt by saying they may have been hesitant to become His followers because they did not know what His real motives were. Perhaps they were thinking He was out to mislead them or to simply make a name for Himself. All of these erroneous thoughts could have been avoided if they had only taken the time to read the Old Testament carefully and compare the writings about the coming Messiah to what Jesus was projecting with His life and His message.

FIND REST FOR YOUR SOUL

I also believe they should have taken a moment to consider that the system they were using at the time, the Mosaic Law, was leading to nothing but personal frustration and

humanistic heartache. They were void of any
real joy in their lives, they were lacking peace,
they had no holy harmony among themselves,
and they were simply going in circles trying to
impose legalistic principles on others that
they were not able to keep themselves. But
when Jesus arrived on the scene, He made
them aware that He had not come to add more
burdens to them, but to lift the load and the
weight of sin from them. That is why He made
statements like, "Come to Me, all you who
labor and are heavy laden, and I will give you
rest. Take My yoke upon you and learn from
Me, for I am gentle and lowly in heart, and
you will find rest for your souls. For My yoke
is easy and My burden is light" (Matthew
11:28–30).

TRY JESUS

Jesus also said, "The thief does not come
except to steal, and to kill, and to destroy. I
have come that they may have life, and that
they may have it more abundantly" (John
10:10). Jesus wanted them to know that if
they were lost, confused, and troubled that He

was the way, the truth, and the light; no man could come to the Father unless they came by Him (John 14:6). This is one of the reasons I can say to people whose lives are empty and troubled that they should try Jesus. I say this boldly and unapologetically because it is evident that what they are trying now is surely not working. There are several reasons I know why it is not working. People are living dejected, defeated, and despondent lives. They have settled for a stale, satanic tuna fish sandwich when the Lord has a lobster-sized blessing with their names on it.

We live among many people who are broken emotionally, bruised physically, bound spiritually, and burdened mentally. They are handicapped to their pasts, handcuffed to their present situations, and hopeless about their futures. There are people all around us who are suffering daily from spiritual starvation, they are dying from divine dehydration, and they are morally malnourished. They are hungry, but the problem is that they are walking right past the blessed banquet feast offered by Jesus.

Unfortunately, they have become satisfied just eating from a satanic garbage can instead.

A BETTER WAY OF LIVING

One of the saddest realities is that this definition also includes a lot of what we call "church people." They come to the feast every Sunday, but all they do is look at the food. They stand in awe of its presentation, and they even compliment the chef. The problem is that they never eat anything the Lord is serving. They talk about how good it smells. They even cry a tear or two about how it is making a difference in the lives of other people. They see how others are growing and getting stronger, but their lack of faith will not allow them to establish a consistent diet of eating the bread from heaven Jesus is offering. They do not realize the Lord is trying to feed them so they will no longer have to live as sickly saints. Instead, they leave many worship experiences, Sunday after Sunday, telling the Lord, No thank You, I'm just not hungry. The main reason they are not hungry could very well be found in the fact that they have polluted their humanistic digestive systems with the devil's demonic groceries. They keep doing this because this is what they have become accustomed to and comfortable with. Then, whenever someone tries to tell them there is a better way of living, including the fact that they can be the head and not the tail, they can become victors and not always victims, they turn a deaf ear and walk away. Because they don't want to change their old way of living.

CONSTANT SATISFACTION

But it is right here in this one verse that Jesus revealed the initial I AM statement about Himself. He gives us another chance to eat, not just from His table and not just from His hand. Jesus gives us an opportunity to eat from the eternal feast that will cause us never to hunger again. These words in John 6:35 are informative, inspirational, and instructional. "And Jesus said to them, 'I am the bread of life.'" Jesus wants the life of each and every one of His true followers to be filled with His *constant satisfaction.*

Jesus made this statement the day after He had finished feeding the multitude of people who numbered more than 20,000, by some estimates. He fed all of them with just two fish and five loaves of bread (John 6:1–14). Jesus was well aware that there were many people who were only following Him to get a reduction on, or an elimination of, their grocery bills. Jesus was passing out free food and they were not about to walk away from this free lunch program. They were only captivated by the physical food so they could feed their bodies, and they had completely overlooked their need to be fed spiritually.

This is still true today. People will work two and three jobs to feed themselves physically, and many of those same people can't remember the last time they were in a ministry meeting, Sunday school, Bible study, or worship service. After eating what their money can buy, they discover they are still hungry. There is still an empty spot and a void in their hearts and souls. An empty spot that only Jesus can fill. Jesus wants to fill that void.

In this story, Jesus had been preaching to these people (v.26–33). He was telling them about the kind of bread they should really chase after. He said to them, "Do not labor for the food which perishes, but for the food which endures to everlasting life, which the Son of Man will give you, because God the Father has set His seal on Him" (v.27). Jesus was trying to get us to understand that the food which satisfies us physically must always be paid for, and we will always have to buy more of it. The food which satisfies us spiritually cannot be afforded by us, but He gives it to us free of charge. Did you not know that when we get a real taste of Jesus, nothing else will ever satisfy us like He can? That is why the psalmist, David, said, "Oh, taste and see that the Lord is good" (Psalm 34:8).

HE'S OUR ALL OR NOTHING LORD

I know there will be some people who will disagree with this next statement I am about to make, but I'm going to say it anyway. I don't believe it is possible for a person to have a real relationship with Jesus Christ, taste from the loaf of His body, eat from His Word, and then walk off from Him and go back to eating out of the devil's hogpen of slop. I believe the church is filled with people who just sample the food the Lord is offering. But the problem lies in the fact that after they sample it, they spit it out after worship and never allow it to become a part of their spiritual digestive systems. They never ingest it.

Allow me to share this simple story with you. On one occasion I was at a restaurant and I wanted a sandwich without any of the pepper sauce they put on the meat. That was when the waiter said to me there was no way he could remove it because it was already mixed in together. And I have discovered that we have many people in the church who want to remove certain things from the loaf of bread Jesus is serving. They are saying, Jesus, I want my loaf without any teaching and preaching about tithing. I want you to cut out the forgiveness; hold the necessity of prayer; leave off any teaching and preaching against adultery, homosexuality, lying, and fornication; and I will take my loaf plain and dry. But Jesus wants us to know that the bread He is serving already has all those ingredients mixed in. You can either eat all of it or not eat any of it at all. The choice is yours.

I have also discovered that it is impossible for us to defend ourselves against the attacks of the devil if we are trying to fight him on an empty stomach, or after removing all the spiritual nutrients that can help us to live victorious lives. Jesus is our *constant satisfaction,* and as long as we keep eating what He is serving, we can be sure all of our spiritual and physical needs will be met.

OUR CONFIDENT STABILIZATION

Jesus went on to say, "He who comes to Me shall never hunger" (v.35). This helped me to realize that Jesus is also our *confident stabilization.* Many of us grow weak and weary in our relationship with the Lord, mainly because we are just not aware of the amount of power He has given to us on the inside. There are also other people who are living in constant defeat and depression because they absolutely refuse to humble themselves to the power and the authority of Jesus Christ. Their lives are filled with one failure after another, but they continue to try to do things their own way. Then there are those people who can testify that the Lord and the Word of the Lord are the only stabilizing forces holding their lives in place.

Somebody reading this book can join in with me and say, If it had not been for the Lord on my side, I don't know where in the world I would be. Somebody else can testify that God's Word has been the one and only constant stabilizing factor in his or her life. Friends have been fickle, employment has been unstable, loved ones are undependable, health is deteriorating, money is funny, change is strange, the transmission is slipping, the roof is leaking, the refrigerator won't get cold, the water heater won't get hot, blood pressure is high, patience is low, the body is weak, and your steps are getting shorter. But in your heart you know God is able because you ate a piece of bread that said,

"'I will never leave you or forsake you'"
(Hebrews 13:5), and that word gave you the
confidence to keep on going. I know it's a
little rough right now; you may be going
through a very dark and dismal period in your
life, but you are still holding on because you
ate a piece of bread that said, "The Lord is my
light and my salvation; whom shall I fear?"
(Psalm 27:1). And that gave you the
confidence to press forward.

HE'S A COMPLETE SERVING

There are enemies trying to attack you from
every direction, but you ate a piece of bread
that said, "Do not fret because of evildoers,
nor be envious of the workers of iniquity. For
they shall soon be cut down like the grass"
(Psalm 37:1). You ate a piece of bread that
said, "No weapon formed against you shall
prosper" (Isaiah 54:17). And now you have
enough strength to hold on just a little while
longer. Jesus wants us to know that when we
come to Him, we will never hunger, because
He alone can satisfy what we really need in

our lives, and that is to be fed from His eternal Word.

Jesus also gives us some additional insight about Himself in this one verse: "He who believes in Me shall never thirst" (v.35). This helps us to embrace the truth that He is a *complete serving.* Jesus begins the verse talking about Himself being the bread of life, but He ends the verse calling our attention to the fact that He also gives us something to quench our thirst. He said, "He who believes in Me shall never thirst." This verse helps me to understand that Jesus promises to give us *restoration* from the brokenness of our past and *refreshment* for our everyday responsibilities. Then He offers a *reward* for our future. It is only in Jesus that we can find this tremendous level of spiritual and physical satisfaction.

I AM THE LIGHT OF THE WORLD

Now early in the morning He came again into the temple, and all the people came to Him; and He sat down and taught them. Then the scribes and Pharisees brought to Him a woman caught in adultery. And when they had set her in the midst, they said to Him, "Teacher, this woman was caught in adultery, in the very act. Now Moses, in the law, commanded us that such should be stoned. But what do You say?" This they said, testing Him, that they might have something of which to accuse Him. But Jesus stooped down and wrote on the ground with His finger, as though He did not hear.

So when they continued asking Him, He raised Himself up and said to them, "He who is without sin among you, let him throw a stone at her first." And again He stooped down and wrote on the ground. Then those who heard it, being convicted by their conscience, went out one by one, beginning with the oldest even to the last. And Jesus was left alone, and the woman standing in the midst. When Jesus had raised Himself up and saw no one but the woman, He said to her, "Woman, where are those accusers of yours? Has no one condemned you?"

She said, "No one, Lord."

And Jesus said to her, "Neither do I condemn you; go and sin no more."

Then Jesus spoke to them again, saying, "I am the light of the world. He who follows Me shall not walk in darkness, but have the light of life."

— John 8:2–12

2

An Illuminating Intervention

Then Jesus spoke to them again, saying, "I AM the light of the world." — John 8:12, emphasis mine

WHEN JESUS MADE this statement, He had just finished doing at least two amazing things in the lives of some people who had had no idea He was about to intervene in their lives in the way He did. First of all, He saved a guilty woman's life.

THEY SET THEIR TRAP

He encountered a woman who was caught in the very act of adultery whom according to the Mosaic Law, deserved a stoning, but Jesus intervened, and in the words of my mother, "He gave her grace and allowed her golden moments to roll on just a little while longer." Then, secondly, He brought extreme embarrassment to all her accusers, and He even forced every one of them to admit to their own personal sinfulness.

We are told in the beginning of John 8 that Jesus was in the temple *very early* in the morning. A great crowd of people came to Him, and He sat down and taught them. Then, suddenly, the scene shifts from the teaching ministry of Jesus to the entrapment schemes of these scribes and Pharisees (John 8:3). We are told Jesus was teaching in the temple, and before He could even get through His introduction and into His first point, these judgmental, hypocritical, duplicitous, busybodies known as the Pharisees showed up. These were men who spent their every waking hour trying to poke holes in the teachings of Jesus. At this point, they were again interrupting the worship and the instruction of Jesus by dragging in a woman whom they claimed they had caught in the very act of adultery.

I want us to pay very close attention to several important factors. First, it was early in the morning when they brought this woman to Jesus. This helps us to understand that these men had been camping out all night long and had stood by and allowed the adultery to take place. They could have intervened and they could have tried to discourage these people from participating in this ungodly activity. It is also suggested by many commentators that these men not only stood by and let it happen, but they also set the trap.

DEALING WITH DISTRACTION

This seems to be a pattern that exists even in our culture. It is puzzling how much effort and energy people will use to entice us to sin and then to catch us in sin, and those same people won't even use one once of their energy to help somebody walk away from sin and into the ways of righteousness.

These men only brought a woman to Jesus who was caught in the act of adultery; however, the last time I checked, it takes a man and a woman to commit this act. I want to know where the man was. We also discover that these men were not really interested in finding out how Jesus would handle a sinful situation and properly apply the Word of God. I say this because I find it strange that they would camp out all night long to catch this woman and use her as a pawn in their evil act of chicanery, but they would not come to the temple with this other group of people who got up early to hear the truth Jesus was preaching. All they wanted to do was expose the weaknesses of somebody else. These scribes and Pharisees represent the people who are still among us today who are only known for interrupting worship and the preaching of the Word of God with some demonic mess and some worthless garbage. These men imposed the teaching of the gospel with the intent to belittle the ministry of Jesus.

This still happens even in our present generation. The devil will do anything and everything he can to try to distract us when the man of God is preaching the Word of God! Cell phones start vibrating and ringing, babies start crying, text notifications start going off, and people will even start talking to you about everything under the sun to keep you from receiving the truth the Lord is trying to deposit in your spirit from His Word.

HE EXPOSES THE HEART

It is evident that these men had set this woman up in an attempt to discredit the Son of God. But Jesus, being the Master of mental manipulation and the motivational mediator of merciful meekness that He is, did not allow the actions of these messy meddlers to catch Him off guard. He did two basic things. First, He took the attention away from the woman when He wrote on the ground and placed the attention on Himself. Then He saved this woman from the public stoning she really deserved (v.3–11). I can truly relate to this, and I hope you can also. Jesus took the attention away from this guilty woman when He wrote on the ground, but He took the attention off guilty sinners like you and me when He hung, bled, and died on an old rugged cross.

Then, secondly, Jesus exposed the internal, sinful, and corrupt nature of each of these scribes and Pharisees when He said, "He who is without sin among you, let him throw a stone at her first" (v.7). That was when their hearts became gripped with guilt. They were convicted by their own consciences and they all dropped their rocks and walked away. The Bible says they left "one by one, beginning with the oldest even to the last" (v.9). Jesus then asked the woman where her accusers were, and she answered by saying they were all gone. He then said to her, "Neither do I condemn you; go and sin no more" (v.11).

Don't focus on the sin

I was greatly inspired by what Jesus did next.
He did not spend a whole lot of time talking
about how guilty this woman was. He did not
waste any more time talking about the evil
heartedness of the scribes and Pharisees. All
He did was go right back to the teaching He
was doing before the interruption initially
began. He said, "I am the light of the world"
(v.12). I wanted to know why Jesus would
mention that He was light right after a
situation like this.

When the accusers are gone

It was then that the Holy Spirit reminded me
that light has several basic characteristics. I
want to deal with at least three of them in this
chapter based in this one verse. When Jesus
said, "I am the light of the world," I believe He
wants us to know that light has the ability to
expose the dirt. Jesus wanted the people
listening to Him teach to know that He is the
kind of light that not only exposes what is

taking place outside our lives, but also the kind of dirt that exists inside our hearts.

I want to ask you to give close consideration to something the Holy Spirit brought to my attention. I believe the reason Jesus did not spend any extra time talking about the dastardly act of the scribes and the Pharisees, and the sins of this woman, was because they were all gone! Wow! Did you catch that? We know the accusers were gone because the Bible tells us in verse 9 that they all left—from the oldest to the youngest—and they left the woman all alone.

Sin no more

Then we know the woman was gone, because Jesus told her to *"Go* and sin no more" (emphasis mine). Look at it again. The apostle John tells us in verses 9–11 that each of the woman's accusers left after Jesus confronted them about their own personal guilt. As a matter of fact, when Jesus asked this woman, "Where are those accusers of yours? Has no one condemned you?" (v.10), she told Him no one had. Then Jesus told her to go and to not become guilty of committing the sinful act again. There is a great principle for us to embrace from this part of the story. The Master did not spend a lot of time dealing with how wrong the men were for trapping this woman. He did not spend a lot of time dealing with how wrong this woman was for committing the act of adultery. Jesus went back to teaching the people who had gotten up early to hear what He had to say to them (v.12). In other words, He dealt with this problem and then went right back to His primary ministry assignment.

FOCUS ON YOUR PRIMARY PURPOSE

This is an area most of us handle incorrectly. We get distracted from what our ministry assignment is, and we start spending more of our time dealing with the problems of people who know in their hearts that they never plan to surrender their lives to the authority of the Word of God.

I must make a confession right here. There are many people who are connected to our congregation at Grace Tabernacle Church

who have felt, at times, that I have had a
passive approach to handling some issues that
came up in and around the church. I have to
remind them that I am not passive; I have just
learned to realize that the devil will do
anything and everything he can to distract me
from my main primary purpose as pastor, and
that purpose is to preach and teach God's
Word to God's people and to pray for them.

My job is to shepherd the Lord's people,
encourage them, correct them when
necessary, and then get right back to what the
Lord has called me to do. I wasn't called to be
a fireman or a spiritual babysitter. My job is to
do what Jesus did. He exposed the dirt in the
hearts of those scribes and Pharisees; He
made the woman aware that what she had
done was wrong. Then He went right back to
preaching the gospel His Father had sent Him
to preach.

Jesus said to them "I am the light of the
world" (v.12). He was making them aware that
He knew about every dirty detail in their lives,
yet He still had the power and the passion to
forgive them and shower them with His grace,

as he does for us. My word of caution to you is to never allow your focus on sinful people and problems to cause you to become stagnated from fulfilling your true ministry responsibilities.

YOU CAN'T JUSTIFY YOUR SIN AROUND JESUS

Jesus went on to say, "He who follows Me shall not walk in darkness" (v.12). The light of Jesus Christ not only exposes the dirt in the hearts of evil men, but it also *eliminates the darkness from our lives.* Notice carefully what Jesus said: "He who follows Me shall not walk in darkness." In other words, those of you who will follow Me will not have to worry about trying to *catch people in their sins* or being *a person who is caught in his or her sins,* but you can become an individual *who helps to deliver people from their sins.* I believe the reason Jesus was not hard on this guilty woman is because she did not make the mistake many of us make when our sins are called to our attention. She did not try to deny her sins, she did not try to defend her sins, and she did not demand that the Lord punish the other person who participated with her in the sin.

Many of us will try to act as if we have not done what we know in our hearts we are guilty of. Then we will try to defend ourselves or justify our actions with excuses or with passing the buck of guilt off on someone else. Then, if those first two don't work, we start to demand that the other people who have sinned with us be brought to justice. But we need to be aware that Jesus has not given us the job of getting specks out of our brother's eye until we learn how to get the beams and logs out of our own eyes. Jesus said, "He who follows Me shall not walk in darkness, but have the light of life" (John 8:12). When we come to Jesus, He will remove us from the darkness of our old way of living and into the light of a loving, lasting, liberating life with our Lord.

HE ELIMINATES ALL THE DARKNESS

I can testify, and I hope you can also, that Jesus turned the light on in my heart once I gave my life sacrificially over to Him. We no longer need to worry about sin catching up with us because Jesus has paid our sin tab in full. We even have a new song in our hearts. It's not I can see clearly now the rain is gone, but I can see clearly now the sin is gone. I can see Jesus moving all the obstacles that were in my way, and since I started following Jesus, it's gonna be a bright, sunshiny day. Jesus is able to *eliminate all the darkness* from our lives.

Jesus closed by saying, "But [he who follows me shall] have the light of life" (v.12). Jesus helps us to understand that He is the great I AM who not only gives us bread to eat, but also light to travel by. He is the light of the world. He *exposed the dirt* in us, He *eliminated the darkness* from us, and He has *established deliverance* for us. He does this in three basic ways. He *leads* us in the right *direction.* He *liberates* us with a new *determination.* He *loves* us with an unconditional *devotion.* He does not love us because of ourselves, but in spite of ourselves. And because Jesus is the light of the whole world, that lets me know He is in a class all by Himself.

His peace is unsurpassable.

His touch is unmistakable.

His power is undeniable.

His wisdom is untraceable.

His radiance is indescribable.

His truth is unshakable.

His word is indestructible.

His mercy is incomprehensible.

His purpose is undefeatable.

His joy inexplicable.

And his love is immeasurable.

He is the light of the world, and He is also the light of my life!

I AM the Door

I am the door of the sheep. All who ever came before Me are thieves and robbers, but the sheep did not hear them. I am the door. If anyone enters by Me, he will be saved, and will go in and out and find pasture.

The thief does not come except to steal, and to kill, and to destroy. I have come that they may have life, and that they may have it more abundantly.

— John 10:7–10

3

COME IN AT THE DOOR

I AM the door of the sheep. — *John 10:7*

THERE IS A SONG we used to sing when I was a child that included the following words. "God has a way that you can't go under, you can't go over, and you can't go around. But you must come in at the door." That song seemed very simple to us when we were children, but today I am made aware of how much biblical and spiritual profundity it truly includes.

COME IN BY THE DOOR

Jesus made this emphatic, bold, and eternal declaration here in John 10. He declared that

He was the door into the sheepfold and all who do not come in by Him, through Him, and/or on Him have not entered properly and will be dealt with accordingly. I find it very interesting that Jesus dealt with the negative aspect of this shepherd and sheep relationship before He even addressed the positive aspects. He began by mentioning those people who do not come in by the door but try to enter by climbing up another way. He referred to them as thieves. "Most assuredly, I say to you, he who does not enter the sheepfold by the door, but climbs up some other way, the same is a thief and a robber" (John 10:1).

HIS WAY IS SIMPLE

Our human nature causes us to do wrong before we will do what is right, so Jesus addresses our human nature before He addresses our spiritual nature. Notice carefully what Jesus made us aware of at the onset. He told us thieves "climb up" (v.9), and later He told us the true sheep don't have to climb, they can just walk in and out and find pasture. This enables us to embrace the truth that climbing requires more energy, effort, and exhaustion. People will go to greater lengths to do things their own way, or the wrong way, while ignoring the simplicity of what the Lord tells them to do. Jesus wants us to know that He is the only true door into an eternal relationship with God. He is not a way, an option, an alternative, or a choice. He is the only way and the only door. But I wanted to know why Jesus would equate Himself with a door.

HE LEADS US INTO UNDERSTANDING

Jesus took the time to explain his story in greater detail to those listening to Him.

> But he who enters by the door is the shepherd of the sheep. To him the doorkeeper opens, and the sheep hear his voice; and he calls his own sheep by name and leads them out. And when he brings out his own sheep, he goes before them; and the sheep follow him, for they know his voice. Yet they will by no means follow a stranger, but will flee from him, for they do not know the voice of strangers." Jesus used this

illustration, but they did not understand the things which He spoke to them.

— John 10:2–6

This helped me to understand that Jesus does not mind us asking Him questions as long as we are prepared to obey when He gives us the answer.

HE IS OUR BRIDGE

We must keep in mind that John 10 is a continuation of thoughts and events spoken to the same crowd from John 9. The blind man had received his sight and Jesus then emphasized that a relationship with Him is not based solely on what He does for us externally, but also on how we are connected to Him internally. The great shepherd, Jesus Christ, has paid the ultimate price for us. We are not our own. We now belong to Him. If He had left us to ourselves, we would have been destroyed by wolves, made destitute of our basic needs, and been disconnected from Him throughout all of eternity. Have you taken the time to consider that the only reason there is a need for a door is because there are walls all around us? This door Jesus spoke about is also the bridge that spans the great gulf between the sinfulness of mankind and the holiness of God. This was Jesus's way of letting us know we no longer have to live under the domain and rule of the devil. God has already paid our fare to cross the bridge into eternity and He is that bridge.

WE KNOW THE SHEPHERD'S VOICE

When Jesus said "All who ever came before Me were thieves and robbers, but the sheep did not hear them" (v.8), He was informing us of at least two important facts. First of all, the sheepfold had experienced an *infiltration of demonic personalities*—plural—thieves and robbers (see Job 1:6). The second thing we see is the *intellect of the sheep.* The rest of the verse says "But the sheep did not hear them." The thieves and robbers were there, but the sheep knew who they should listen to. These sheep were sensitive to the voice of their shepherd because they had a relationship with Him. Do you know your shepherd's voice well enough not to listen to the voice of the enemy when he attempts to lead you astray?

The thieves that climbed up the walls represent those people who enter in the earthly gathering of God's people called the local church. These are the people who creep in among us who have wolf-like and goat-like mindsets. They are dressed properly on the outside, but they lack a true internal spiritual transformation. But the door that bridges the gap between sin and salvation is the eternal door, and it can only be crossed and entered by those who express true saving faith in Jesus Christ.

JESUS IS THE WAY INTO ABUNDANT LIFE

Jesus promises that when we enter the door into an eternal relationship with Him, we will experience *security*. He said we "will be saved" (v.9). Then we will also experience *sustenance*. We can go in and out and we will find pasture. Pastures represent fertile places—places where new seed can be planted, new fruit can grow, and new opportunities can blossom. Then we will experience *salvation*. The thief comes to kill, steal, and destroy, but Jesus has come to offer us not just an earthly existence, but also life abundantly. He says we can have it because He has already paid for it!

I AM THE GOOD SHEPHERD

I am the good shepherd. The good shepherd gives His life for the sheep. But a hireling, he who is not the shepherd, one who does not own the sheep, sees the wolf coming and leaves the sheep and flees; and the wolf catches the sheep and scatters them. The hireling flees because he is a hireling and does not care about the sheep. I am the good shepherd; and I know My sheep, and am known by My own. As the Father knows Me, even so I know the Father; and I lay down My life for the sheep. And other sheep I have which are not of this fold; them also I must bring, and they will hear My voice; and there will be one flock and one shepherd.

— John 10:11–16

4

THE GOOD SHEPHERD

I am the good shepherd. The good shepherd
gives His life for the sheep. — John 10:11

ALLOW ME TO BEGIN this chapter by informing
us that we, as believers in Jesus Christ and
children of God, have so much to rejoice about
and so much to thank the Lord for. I believe
one of the reasons many of us walk around
with sad dispositions and melancholy attitudes
is because we just don't know how blessed we
really are.

HE WATCHES OVER US

One of the many things which should bring a tremendous amount of joy and comfort to our hearts is that we are the Lord's sheep and Jesus Christ is our protecting, providing, and passionate shepherd. I realize this may sound simplistic on the surface, but the deeper profundity of the matter lies in the facts that the Lord never expects any of His sheep to protect themselves, provide for themselves, or promote themselves. The Lord is our loving, heavenly Father and He has not only created us, He also sent His Son, Jesus Christ, into the world as a perfect sacrifice for us. Because He has died for our sins and He has been raised from the grave for our salvation, He wants us to know He accepts full responsibility for us. Jesus is the one whom God has assigned to lead us, guide us, guard us, and govern every phase and aspect of our lives.

HE NURTURES AND NOURISHES US

Since we have surrendered to Him, we are now a part of His divine sheepfold. If you

don't believe me, then just take a fresh look at
the end of Psalm 100:3. It is there that we
read these words, "We are His people and the
sheep of His pasture." We have been "bought
with a price" (1 Corinthians 6:20), and we are
being protected by His amazing grace and His
mercies that are "new every morning"
(Lamentations 3:23). Notice carefully what
the psalmist said: We are not just His sheep,
but we are also the sheep of His pasture. This
word "pasture" literally means the feeding
place where the Lord nurtures and nourishes
all of His sheep. This is God's way of
reminding us that as long as we remain in the
sheepfold, we will never go hungry and all our
basic needs will be met.

HE'LL BRING YOU SAFELY HOME

When the Lord calls us *His people,* this simply
means God has made us as individuals and He
has given us the ability to make choices. But
when He calls us *His sheep,* this helps us to
realize the Lord is also aware that His people
often make decisions that lead them into some
dreadful and difficult situations. The Lord

knows there are some sheep who are a part of His fold who became distracted and wandered away while eating without looking up. Others were led away by a demonic influence when they took their eyes off their shepherd. But in spite of it all, Jesus Christ is the kind of shepherd who will go looking for His sheep, and He will not suspend His search until He finds every one of us who has been called by His name.

Can you rejoice that the Lord loved you enough to come looking for you, even after you had strayed away from the fold? We need to be reminded that you were safe and secure in His arms but allowed other people, positions, problems and/or pain to separate you from Him. But, in spite of it all, Jesus showed up right where you were. He put you back on His shoulders, and you are still alive today because the Lord loved you enough to bring you safely back home.

JESUS PERSONALIZED THE RELATIONSHIP

Here in John 10, Jesus had just finished telling those He was teaching that He was the door that leads into the sheepfold. We are informed that every person who does not come in by Him is a thief and a robber. Then He personalized the relationship even more and took it to an even higher level of intimacy when He said, "I am the good shepherd." I want you to notice the ascending level of closeness the Lord has with His people. He told us, "I am the door of the sheep" (v.7), but Jesus knew a door can be considered as an inanimate object with no feelings, no flexibility, and no faithfulness. A door can be viewed as lacking in reciprocal interactions. So He moved to a new plateau by personalizing the relationship with His people when He said, "I am the good shepherd" (v.11). This was Jesus's way of establishing that He knows we all need somebody to lead us.

GOOD LEADERS MAKE OUR LIVES MORE MEANINGFUL

He also knows that if we do not choose the right leader, we will wind up following ungodly and irresponsible leadership:

leadership that will cause us to find ourselves in positions of doom, destruction, and death. As the door, Jesus serves as the way into a new relationship with God, but as our shepherd, He assumes full responsibility for our everyday protection. When we consider what Jesus warned us against and what He is offering, I cannot even imagine why anybody would not choose to follow Him. He said, "The thief does not come but for to steal, and to kill and to destroy, I have come that they may have life and have it more abundantly" (v.10).

Jesus has not come to make our lives more miserable but to make our lives more meaningful. Jesus has come to show us the way out of our dark, helpless, and hopeless situations. Jesus has come to add purpose, peace, praise, and protection to our lives. Jesus has come to move us beyond simply going through the motions of ecclesiastical and gymnastic religiosity. He has come to show us that life with God is not about devotion to a routine but about developing a relationship. We need to take a moment to reflect and ask ourselves who we are following, why we are following them, and how our lives have become better since we have been loyal, devoted, and committed to what we are attached to.

WE CHOOSE JESUS

"I am the *good shepherd*" (v.11, emphasis mine). When Jesus said this, He was making us aware that there are other shepherds we have the option of choosing, but none of them can offer what He has to offer.

I also believe this was His way of setting the record straight by letting us know that it does not make sense to choose Him and then start to complain about the direction in which He is leading us. Jesus wants us to know that following Him is a choice we make and not something we are forced into.

When He uses this word "good," it means He is a valuable, virtuous, better, honest, and worthy shepherd and leader. Notice what Jesus was doing. He treasures His sheep so much that He also takes the time and the effort to be meticulously detailed in His explanation and His presentation of Himself.

Jesus is the Son of God who owns all things
and rules all things. He is the sum total of all
perfection, yet He was taking the time and
trying to convince scum of the earth, like you
and me, why we should choose Him over some
other shepherds who ultimately only mean us
harm.

Instead of us begging a perfect Jesus to
accept worthless sinners like us, we have a
perfect Jesus trying to persuade worthless
sinners to accept Him. Jesus wanted us to
know we are not simply following some
novice, some upstart, some Johnny-come-
lately. He is the King of Kings and the Lord of
Lords. He is the Ancient of Days, the creator
of all things, and the sustainer of everything
He has made. He is the "be" in let there be. He
is the platform of the past that holds us in
place for the present and secures our positions
in the future. He is the spoken Word from the
mouth of God, the living Word from the heart
of God, and the eternal Word from the mind
of God. He is the shepherd who has never
abandoned any of His sheep. Here, He was
pleading with His own people He made with

His hand to trust Him to lead and guide every step of their lives.

HE IS OUR SACRIFICE

He is a sacrificial shepherd. The reason I know this to be true is because the verse goes on to say, "The good shepherd gives His life for the sheep" (v.11). This is what I want to call a panoramic paradox, an incredible irony, and an outstanding oxymoron from the Old Testament; because according to the old Levitical Law, the sheep would have to die for the sins of the shepherds. But Jesus said that system had failed for more than two thousand years and His people were still living with the burden of their sins; so he was going to flip the script, and instead of His people killing an innocent lamb every time they sinned, He was going to offer to shed every drop of His innocent blood so we wouldn't have to suffer the penalty of our sins. "The good shepherd gives His life for the sheep." His life was not taken from Him. He was not murdered, He was not assassinated, He was not mugged, He was not cross jacked. He gave His life for us, although none of us deserved what He was offering. How in the world can we possibly complain and not have confidence in Jesus when we have a shepherd willing to do all of this and more for us? He is a shepherd who has all of these positive qualities. He is a shepherd who loves us so much that He will die in our place so that we can live with Him throughout all of eternity, and it does not cost us one dime.

JESUS IS CONSISTENT IN HIS COMPANIONSHIP

Jesus told us what our other choices are. He helped us to understand that a hireling is a person who will leave the sheep when he sees a wolf coming simply to save himself. The hireling does not own the sheep, which means he has not paid anything for the sheep. He is not interested in giving to the sheep, but only in getting what he can from the sheep. The hireling does not care about the sheep. "'But a hireling, he who is not the shepherd, one who does not own the sheep, sees the wolf coming and leaves the sheep and flees; and the wolf catches the sheep and scatters them. The hireling flees because he is a hireling and does not care about the sheep'" (v.12). We need to learn the importance of being *confident in the choice* we have made, and then we need to learn that Jesus is *consistent in His companionship.*

The hireling is only with the sheep in order to get paid. But Jesus is the shepherd who pays so He can spend more time with undeserving, hardheaded, stiff-necked, and rebellious sheep.

HE KEEPS ON LOVING US

Whenever there is a separation in the relationship between us and the Lord, it is never because He left us; it is always because we left Him. This question may help you in understanding the profundity of these words spoken by our Savior. How many of you would keep on loving people, forgiving people, providing for people, and making a way for people who ignored you, robbed you, let you down, broke your heart, disobeyed your commandments, violated your word, used your body for their pleasure, and never gave you glory? Yet this is exactly what we have done to the Lord, but in spite of it all, He just keeps on loving us and pouring His grace out on us.

Jesus is not a hireling because He does not run and hide when He sees the wolf coming. As a matter of fact, the wolf runs and hides whenever it sees Jesus coming. Jesus has prayed for his sheep. He knows His sheep by name. Jesus said, "The hireling flees because he is a hireling and does not care about the sheep." There are some people who come into our lives and all they are concerned about is our doing what is best for them and never about us working collectively to bring glory to the Lord. The thief comes to steal, kill, and destroy. The hireling runs off whenever trouble comes in his or her direction.

HE KNOWS US AND WE FOLLOW HIM

But then He gives us the epitome of what a real, genuine shepherd looks like. He said, "I am the good shepherd; and I know My sheep, and am known by My own. As the Father knows Me, even so I know the Father; and I lay down My life for the sheep" (v.14–15).

That is where I want to leave you. We need to have *confidence in the choice* we have made in a shepherd. We need to know Jesus is *consistent in His companionship* as our shepherd. He will never leave us. But finally, we also are made aware that our shepherd offers us a *crucifixion connection.*

A CRUCIFIXION CONNECTION

When I looked carefully at verses 14 and 15, at least two things leaped from the pages:

- Jesus is a shepherd who has a *relationship with all His sheep.* He said, "I know My sheep, and My sheep know Me." Jesus desires to have a greater level of intimacy with each of His sheep.

- Jesus fulfills His *responsibility to His sheep.* He knows this is an assignment His Father God has given to Him. That is why He said, "As the Father knows Me, even so I know the Father." He did not want to fail His Father in heaven.

Jesus has *redeemed all His sheep.* He said, "I lay down My life for the sheep" Jesus knew no man could take His life, but He willingly laid it down. He died for us and He was buried for us, but early Sunday morning, He rose from the grave for us.

I Am the Resurrection and the Life

*When Jesus came, He found that [Lazarus]
had already been in the tomb four days. Now
Bethany was near Jerusalem, about two miles
away. And many of the Jews had joined the
women around Martha and Mary, to comfort
them concerning their brother.*

*Then Martha, as soon as she heard that Jesus
was coming, went and met Him, but Mary was
sitting in the house. Now Martha said to
Jesus, "Lord, if You had been here, my
brother would not have died. But even now I
know that whatever You ask of God, God will
give You."*

*Jesus said to her, "Your brother will rise
again."*

*Martha said to Him, "I know that he will rise
again in the resurrection at the last day."*

*Jesus said to her, "I am the resurrection and
the life. He who believes in Me, though he*

may die, he shall live. And whoever lives and believes in Me shall never die.

— John 11:17–26

5

FINDING LIFE IN A DEAD SITUATION

He who believes in Me, though he may die, he shall live. — John 11:25

WHENEVER JESUS TAKES THE TIME to speak to His people, He is always careful and meticulous to do at least two prominent things:

- First, He is concerned enough to share words of correction that will help us to see the errors in our lives that need to be changed. Jesus knows we will never become all we should be, or all we can be, as long as we are living outside His will for our lives.

- Secondly, He is loving enough to share words of comfort that will meet us at our specific points of need and at the most important areas of our lives. After Jesus corrects us, challenges us, and confronts us about our sins, shortcomings, and transgressions, He then expresses His compassion toward us. That is when He loves us back into a healthy and wholesome relationship with Himself.

HE MEETS US IN OUR PLACE OF NEED

Throughout the Gospel of John, we once again find Jesus following this same pattern. It is here we see Jesus as He shared what has been classified and categorized as the I AM statements of the Master. When we take the time to carefully examine the four statements preceding the one in this chapter, we will make an amazing discovery. What we will discover is that each one of His I AM statements meets us in the places we need the

Lord the most in our lives. In other words,
when Jesus speaks, He does not simply ramble
with an overexaggerated use of words to
impress us with His intellect and His verbiage.
Instead, every word that comes out of His
mouth is designed to help us, heal us, give
hope to us, and hide us from the hurt Satan
desires to use to harm us.

Every one of His I AM statements touches
us physically and elevates our trust in Him
spiritually. If you have any doubt in your mind
about this, then just take a moment to review
the previous I AM statements.

- When Jesus said, "I am the bread of
  life" (John 6:35), this shows us how He
  speaks to our basic need for physical
  and spiritual nourishment. He was
  reinforcing that man cannot live by
  bread alone, but we need every word
  which proceeds from the mouth of God.

- When He said, "I am the light of the
  world" (John 8:12), this shows us His
  recognition that without Him, we are
  all doomed for defeat by the demonic
  darkness. He is the Lord of luminosity,

and He lightens our pathway even when we are forced to walk through the valley of the shadow of death.

- When Jesus said, "I am the door of the sheep" (John 10:7), this helps us to recognize that He is the only way for us to enter into the presence of the almighty God and experience eternal salvation. He is not *a* way or *one of many* ways; He holds the rights on eternal exclusivity into the presence of His heavenly Father.

- Then when He said, "I am the good shepherd" (John 10:11), this helps us to see that Jesus not only feeds us (John 6:35), He not only illuminates our path (John 8:12), He not only provides a passage for us to get to God (John 10:7), but He also accepts full and complete responsibility for us by claiming us as His own sheep. He is the shepherd who lays down His life for each and every one of those who are a part of His divine sheepfold.

FINDING LIFE IN THE MIDST OF DEATH

It is here, in John 11:25, that Jesus confronted what most of us would consider to be our greatest fear: the fear of death and dying. Jesus knows this is the one thing that hinders most of us from trusting Him, surrendering to Him, obeying Him, remaining committed to Him, and even believing everything we have heard from Him. This passage takes place after the death of His dear friend Lazarus. I will not attempt to address the entire story in minute and microscopic exegetical detail, but I will share with you what the Holy Spirit has shared with me about how we can learn to start finding life even in the midst of some dead situations.

JESUS COULD HAVE...

Lazarus took sick and it appeared to his sisters, Mary and Martha, that this sickness was leading to his death. Being hopeful, they sent for Jesus (John 11:1–3). But an amazing thing happened (v.6). We are told that when Jesus heard about this sickness, He stayed two more days where He was before He even went to see about Lazarus. Before Jesus arrived on the scene, Lazarus died. Now, those of us who read the Bible on a regular basis know that Jesus could have come to the home and saved Lazarus from death. We even know Jesus could have just spoken the word and Lazarus could have been healed. We even know that if some people had picked up Lazarus and brought him to Jesus, He could have healed him on the spot. But the Master did not do any of these things, nor did He cause any of these things to take place.

WHY JESUS DELAYS

The first question we need to seek an answer for is why Jesus delayed His arrival at the home of Lazarus. In addition, we should also consider why Jesus seems to delay coming to see about us when we think we need Him the most. One of my daughters in ministry, Rev. Vandra Noel, helped me in a way even she may not realize. She helped me to understand that there are times when Jesus delays His arrival to give us a greater appreciation of His presence when He does show up.

Jesus knows we tend to take Him for granted, so there are times when He will delay just to get a greater *hallelujah* out of us, a stronger *praise the Lord* out of us, or a more sincere *thank you, Jesus* from us. Then there are other times when Jesus will delay just to see if we will try to solve the problem ourselves. He may wait to see if we choose what seem to be other unworkable alternatives.

Will you start drinking, drugging, doping, doubting, and destroying yourself with poor choices and giving in to demonic suggestions? What do you turn to when Jesus does not show up in your situation when you think He should? His delay will often reveal who we really are and who we really trust.

HE'LL SHOW UP ON TIME

The story of Lazarus helps us to understand that there will be times when Jesus will delay because He already knows the time He has planned for our deliverance. He knows exactly what He is going to do for us and when.

No matter how desperate we become, the truth of the matter is, in the words of our fore-parents: You can't hurry God, no, you have just got to wait. He may not come when you want Him to, but when He does show up, He will be right on time.

When Jesus did make His arrival, Martha met Him before He even got to the house and said to Him, "Lord, if you had been here, my brother would not have died" (v.21). Jesus said two basic things to her. His first statement was, "Your brother will rise again" (v.23). Then He said, "I am the resurrection" (v.25). As much as we may not want to face it, here Jesus is forcing us to accept the certainty of death.

SOME STUFF NEEDS TO DIE

While you are pondering that, allow me to share this: There cannot be an ascending from the grave unless there has first been a descending into the grave. In other words, Jesus cannot raise us to walk in the newness of life until He has allowed some old things we are holding onto to die out. Many of us have become attached to and committed to some stuff that needs to die before Jesus can show us the real joy of abundant living.

I believe one of the reasons many people are not more committed to the Lord than they are is because they are trying to keep some stuff alive—things Jesus knows need to die in their lives. It is hard to be committed when you are carrying around deadweight every day of your life, because deadweight is heavy weight, and it hinders us from moving at the pace the Lord desires from us. That is why the apostle Paul said, "Let us lay aside every weight, and the sin which so easily ensnares us, and let us run with endurance the race that is set before us, looking unto Jesus, the author and finisher of our faith" (Hebrews 12:1–2).

Death represents a seed that is planted, but resurrection represents a bountiful harvest that comes forth at a later season in our lives. Jesus said to Martha, "I am the resurrection." In other words, the situation may be too dead

for you, but it is just right for Him. I want to
encourage you with the truth that there are
some things that must die out of our lives
before new things are going to be able to
grow, bloom, and blossom in our lives.

JESUS MUST COME FIRST

Jesus also said, "I am the life" (v.25). Even
though there is the certainty of death, we also
need to have confidence in His deliverance.
When Jesus said, "I am the resurrection," this
means He can make you alive again. But when
He added, "I am the life," this means He can
keep you alive throughout all of eternity. We
need to know there will be times when the
Lord will allow some things to die in and
around our lives, and not always because they
are negative and destructive things.
Sometimes He will allow things in our lives to
die because they have become *distractive*
things. Those are the things that hinder us
from hearing God's voice and doing God's
will. It may not be drugs, alcohol, gambling,
or adultery, but it could be a job you are more
attached to than you are to Jesus Christ, or a

new relationship that has blinded and
distracted you from seeing Jesus. You are
fulfilling your responsibilities to them and you
have forsaken your responsibilities to Him.
Does any of this sound familiar?

DELIGHT IN HIM

The Lord will allow some things we desire to
have (more than we *desire* Him) to die in our
lives. We work hard to get those things, but
we need to ask ourselves how hard we are
working to improve our relationship with
Jesus Christ. "Delight yourself also in the
Lord, and He shall give you the desires of your
heart" (Psalm 37:4). This verse helped me to
understand that the only way we can get the
things we want is to make the Lord the
number one priority in our lives. Until we do
this, He will continue to allow one thing after
another to die out around us.

DEPEND ON HIM

Then there are things the Lord will allow to
die that we *depend* on more than we depend

on Him. God is a jealous God, and He does not want His children depending on any people, possessions, positions, or promises more than we depend on Him. He is the only God who is able to provide not some, but all, of our needs. This is what you call abundant life. The Christian life is not just limited to getting up out of our dead situations, but also about staying up. This means even when we die physically, we do not lose; instead, we gain more than we have ever experienced before. Paul said it like this: "For to me, to live is Christ, and to die is gain" (Philippians 1:21).

BELIEVE IN HIM

Then, finally, Jesus said, "He who believes in Me, though he may die, he shall live" (v.25). And that is where Jesus calms our hearts about the *certainty of death.* He comforts our hearts with the *confidence of His deliverance.* But then He challenges our hearts with a *commitment to His doctrine.*

When you are faced with a crucial decision, whose doctrine are you going to believe? The Sadducees claimed there was no resurrection from the dead. Do you believe in the teachings of the atheists, who say that when we die, we are done? Do you believe in the teaching of the agnostics, who are uncertain about what happens to people after they die? Or do you believe in Jesus, who said, "He who believes in Me, though he may die, he shall live." This statement allows us to embrace at least three basic things.

- First, death is not *final.* Jesus will have the last word.
- Secondly, death does not have to be *feared,* because we know that just as the Lord walks with us through life, He will also walk with us through death.
- Thirdly, we need to know that our *faith* will carry us through death.

The Bible says, "If we endure, we shall also reign with Him" (2 Timothy 2:12). My faith helps me to understand that because He has died for my eternal punishment, I can handle the temporary sleep until I enter into His glorious presence.

I AM THE WAY, THE TRUTH, AND THE LIFE

Let not your heart be troubled; you believe in God, believe also in Me. In My Father's house are many mansions; if it were not so, I would have told you. I go to prepare a place for you. And if I go and prepare a place for you, I will come again and receive you to Myself; that where I am, there you may be also. And where I go you know, and the way you know."

Thomas said to Him, "Lord, we do not know where You are going, and how can we know the way?"

Jesus said to him, "I am the way, the truth, and the life. No one comes to the Father except through Me."

— John 14:2–6

6

JESUS IS ALL THAT

Jesus said to him, "I am the way, the truth, and the life. No one comes to the Father except through Me." — John 14:6

THE OTHER DAY while sitting in a restaurant, I happened to overhear a conversation between two young ladies about a problem one of them was having with her boyfriend. She was telling her friend about all the demands he was placing on her, all the drama he was causing her to experience, and all the heartache and pain she was going through since he had become a part of her life. She continued to tell her friend that he thought he was God's gift to women. Then she finally said, "Girl, I just had to tell him, 'Hold on there, brother, because I don't know who you think I am, but you sure ain't all that.'" I guess this was her way of saying to him, I can do a whole lot better, and you leave a lot to be desired in a good quality boyfriend. This woman was speaking out of her frustration, because evidently the man she was with had not lived up to her expectations of him when their relationship first started.

HE GIVES US THE RELATIONSHIP WE HOPED FOR

I am sure most of us can relate to being hurt by people who have not fulfilled the promises they made to us when we first met them. If we had a chance to confront some of those people, we would probably say to them, just like that lady at the restaurant, You ain't all that. But when I look at the life of Jesus and consider not only what He has said about Himself, but also what others who truly know Him have had to say about their experiences with Him, I

believe I should have some witnesses to join
me in saying Jesus is *all that*.

It is right here that Jesus spoke to the man
we have come to know as doubting Thomas. "I
am the way, the truth, and the life. No one
comes to the Father except through Me"
(John 14:6). This seems to be the Master's way
of saying he is our only hope for getting
reconnected with God, and without Him, we
are doomed for eternal damnation.

JESUS PLANS AHEAD

This verse is a part of what commentators call
the Upper Room Discourse between Jesus and
His twelve disciples. It started in John 13 and
it continues through the end of John 17. Jesus
was aware that He was less than twenty-four
hours away from crucifixion, less than three
days away from resurrection, and less than
fifty-three days away from His ascension back
to heaven—where He would be seated at the
right-hand side of His Father. Jesus was about
to leave the work and the responsibility of
winning the world back to God in the hands of
these men. He also knew that before the

weekend was over, one of them would deny Him, one would betray Him, and after His resurrection, one would doubt Him. As if that wasn't enough, He also knew they would all forsake Him. But we find Him here taking the time to share some priceless and precious principles with them. It is because He already knew He had restoration grace for every one of them after His resurrection from the grave.

In this Upper Room Discourse, Jesus was no longer focusing on healing the sick, giving sight to the blind, providing walking ability for the lame, or casting out demonic spirits. His focus was not even exclusively centered on the arrest He was about to submit to, the lies that were about to be told on Him, the agony He was about to endure, the humiliation He was about to undergo, nor the crucifixion He was about to suffer. Now, even though Jesus was about to face the most excruciating and painful period in His humanistic existence, we will discover that in this discourse, His focus was not on what He was about to endure but on preparing His disciples for the work ahead of them.

MAKING PROMISES WHILE HURT

Jesus had already made them aware of the harsh treatment He was about to endure and that He was going to a place they would not be able to travel to with Him, but He said they would be able to go there later. It was then "Peter said to Him, 'Lord, why can I not follow You now? I will lay down my life for Your sake' Jesus answered him, 'Will you lay down your life for My sake? Most assuredly, I say to you, the rooster shall not crow till you have denied Me three times'" (John 13:37–38).

Jesus knew that when we have hurting hearts, and during times of emotional uncertainty, we will often make statements without being prepared to fulfill them; we will make promises with our mouths we are unable to keep with our lives. So Jesus began with what we have come to know as one of His most comforting, heartwarming, reassuring, and encouraging statements. "'Let not your heart be troubled; you believe in God, believe also in Me'" (John 14:1).

Jesus went on to tell them His Father's house has many mansions and He was going away to start making preparations for their later arrival. He also told them He was going to come back and get them so they would be able to spend eternity in the same place He would be living.

WHAT'S YOUR AGENDA?

Then Jesus made what I consider to be an unusual statement. I wanted to know what Jesus was trying to get His disciples to understand when He made this statement. He said, "And where I go you know, and the way you know" (v.4). This was perplexing to me, because Jesus had just said to them, "Where I am going you cannot follow Me now, but you shall follow Me afterward" (John 13:36). They did, in fact, know where He was going, and they also knew the way to get there.

When Peter asked Him why he could not follow Him (John 13:37), Jesus responded with a word of rebuke to expose Peter's impending failure. But just a few verses later, when Thomas said, "Lord, we do not know

where You are going, and how can we know
the way?" Jesus responded with a word of
reassurance and a word of direction. What
was the difference? The answer is found in the
motives behind the two questions. Peter said,
"Lord why can't *I* follow You now? *I* will lay
down *my* life for You." But Thomas said, " *We*
do not know where You are going, and how
can *we* know the way?" The difference is
Peter had a selfish agenda while Thomas was
concerned about *all* the disciples traveling in
the right direction. Peter was expressing his
arrogance while Thomas was looking for
assurance. Peter was showing his *pride,* but
Thomas was seeking the right *pathway.* Peter
was trying to *boast,* but Thomas was trying to
strengthen his *belief.* Peter was trying to
showcase his superior superciliousness, but
Thomas was *simply seeking strength from the
Savior.*

Jesus rebuked Peter to let him know that
when you are selfish and try to do it all by
yourself, you will fail every time. But when
you are like Thomas and want to make sure
everybody is traveling in the same direction,

Jesus will take the time to answer your question, and He will provide comfort and reassurance.

THERE ARE NO STUPID QUESTIONS TO JESUS

Notice that Jesus did not condemn Thomas for this question; He did not even criticize his ignorance. He simply said to him, "I am the way, the truth and the life. No one comes to the Father except through Me" (John 14:6). I believe this was His way of saying I AM *all that!* I AM the pathway to redemption.

When Jesus said, "I am the way, the truth, and the life," I believe this was His way of informing us that there are no limits to Him, no restrictions on Him, and no boundaries beyond Him. But for the sake of clarity, let's meticulously and analytically dissect and methodically approach this one verse in the order that Jesus spoke it.

The first thing He chose to reveal to Thomas about Himself was that *He is the way.* This helped me to understand that many of us are living frustrating and nonproductive lives because we are too busy pursuing what we think we can get from Jesus, as opposed to what He can receive from us. We should be focused on trying to discover who Jesus is and the direction He wants us to go.

Jesus said, "I am the way." The Master wanted us to know that as long as we are following Him, we are guaranteed of at least three things. First, following in His way means:

- ✓ we will never get *lost,*
- ✓ we will never get *lonely,* and
- ✓ we will always be *loved.*

HE IS THE ONLY WAY

When Jesus said, "I am the way," He was speaking to the fact that He knows the only time we make some of the greatest mistakes in our lives is when we stop following Him. He knows that when we get lost, we will do some terrible things and take advice from anybody we run into. Losing our way then leads to desperation, and desperation causes us to travel down some evil pathways. Then Jesus knows that when we are *lonely,* we have a strong tendency to gravitate to some people

who may mean us more harm than good. We
get into unhealthy and ungodly relationships,
and it is all because we have stopped following
in His ways. Then Jesus also knows that when
we feel *unloved,* we will do harm to ourselves.
We will fail to recognize the value He has
placed upon us and allow other people to
abuse us and take advantage of us. In the
words of Waylon Jennings' song "Looking for
Love," we start looking for love in all the
wrong places. But Jesus wants us to know that
He is the only way to make sure we never get
lost. He is the only way to make sure we never
get lonely, and He is the only way to make
sure we will always experience His love. When
Jesus said He is the way, this helps us to
realize that no matter how many bumps,
potholes, construction, delays, and detours we
may experience, all we have to do is keep
following Him and we will make it to our
heavenly home. Jesus does not simply point
the way or teach the way; He is the way.

HE IS THE ONLY TRUTH

Not only does He say, "I am the way." He also says, "I am the truth." Jesus is not only the pathway to righteousness, He also gives us the principles for righteousness. Jesus knows that while we are traveling on the road, we need some guidance to make sure we don't get distracted by the detours. The Lord knows there will be times when troubles and difficulty may blind us from seeing Him, and that is when we need to make sure we are following the roadmap of His truth.

There will be times in our lives when we don't always feel like praying, but His Word of truth says, "Men always ought to pray and not lose heart" (Luke 18:1). There will be times when you don't always feel like lifting holy hands and giving glory to God, but His Word of truth says, "Let everything that has breath praise the Lord" (Psalm 150:6).

There will be times when we can't see Jesus clearly, when we want to get even with that person who hurt us and betrayed us, but His Word of truth says, "Love your enemies, bless those who curse you, do good to those who hate you, and pray for those who spitefully use you and persecute you" (Matthew 5:44).

I know there will be times in life when our money is funny and our change is strange. We will want to pay light bills and car notes before we pay the Lord, but His Word of truth says, "'Bring all the tithes into the storehouse, that there may be food in My house, and try Me now in this,' says the Lord of hosts, 'if I will not open for you the windows of heaven and pour out for you such blessing that there will not be room enough to receive it" (Malachi 3:10). His Word of truth is the divine GPS—not the Global Positioning System but the Godly Plan of Salvation, and it guides us and helps us to make sure we never become disconnected from Him.

HIS TRUTH GUIDES, GUARDS, AND GOVERNS US

This word "truth" (v.6) in terms of Jesus being the truth literally means he is the originator and the ultimate example of the legitimacy. This is not just a title Jesus assumes; this is the very essence of His being. There is no lying, no dishonesty, no variation, no vacillation, no deviation, no fluctuation, or instability in Him. Jesus is not just a God who does not lie, He is a God who *cannot* lie. It is the one thing He lacks the ability to do. When He said "I am the truth," He was making us aware that with Him, we have the ultimate example of honesty and proficiency. But without Him we are forced to accept one lie after another.

1. The truth He gives to us *guides* us. It leads us in the right direction.
2. It *guards* us, it prevents the devil from eternally destroying us.
3. It *governs* us as well by making sure we are given sound, godly information.

HE IS OUR ONLY LIFE

Jesus closed by saying, "I am the life. No one comes to the Father except through Me" (v.6). Jesus is the pathway to righteousness, Jesus gives us the principles for redemption, and only Jesus has the power for reconnection. This helped me to understand that Jesus was

saying I am *all that,* because I am the only one
who knows how to get you reconnected to
God. We were expurgated from His presence
when Adam and Eve were driven out of the
garden of Eden because of their sinful
disobedience, but Jesus said he was about to
lead them to a new path that would show
them, and us, how to get back to Him. They
had tried other paths and none of them had
worked. He is the only way.

You have tried the way of *materialism* only
to discover that money cannot buy you
happiness. You have tried the way of
education only to discover that education
without salvation leads to ruination. But Jesus
said He was inviting us to follow Him up a
new path, which is the way to Calvary. He said
we can only go so far, and when we get to the
bottom of the hill, we can just step back and
watch Him climb the hill for our sins and
show us how much He really loves us. All we
have to do is believe and then lead others back
to the place where He has led us. He died for
us, but early on Sunday morning, God raised
Jesus from the grave. And today He is still

able to raise us from any and all dead situations that seem to be staring us in the face. If we have the believing faith, God has the resurrection power.

I AM THE TRUE VINE

*I am the true vine, and My Father is the
vinedresser. Every branch in Me that does not
bear fruit He takes away; and
every branch that bears fruit He prunes, that
it may bear more fruit. You are already clean
because of the word which I have spoken to
you. Abide in Me, and I in you. As the branch
cannot bear fruit of itself, unless it abides in
the vine, neither can you, unless you abide in
Me.*

*I am the vine, you are the branches. He who
abides in Me, and I in him, bears much fruit;
for without Me you can do nothing. If anyone
does not abide in Me, he is cast out as a
branch and is withered; and they gather them
and throw them into the fire, and they are
burned. If you abide in Me, and My
words abide in you, you will ask what you
desire, and it shall be done for you. By this My
Father is glorified, that you bear much
fruit; so you will be My disciples.*

— John 15:1–8

7

PERFECTLY POSTURED FOR PRODUCTIVITY

He who abides in Me, and I in him, bears
much fruit. — John 15:1–5

I BELIEVE ONE of the prominent things Jesus
wants to establish in the heart, soul, and mind
of every follower of His is the knowledge that
He is the sum total for all our humanistic and
eternal needs. It is imperative to Him that
every person who has ever placed his or her
trust and confidence in Him be assured that
He not only has everything we need, but also
that He is everything we need now and will
ever need in the future.

GOD'S UNLIMITED ABUNDANCE

Jesus does not want us living in fear and wondering if there are some aspects of our lives we can only have fulfilled and satisfied outside His provision. He is not just a God who desires to conciliate our immediate wants and appease our instant desires, but He is also able to meet our future needs, even throughout all of eternity.

Jesus knows people have a tendency to isolate Him and compartmentalize Him into some small boxes or some limited area of their comfort zones. We want Him to take care of all we would consider to be the religious stuff in our lives, and then we can rely and depend on other resources for the decisions that need to be made when we are beyond the four walls of what we call the church house.

LORD OF ALL OR NOT AT ALL

But we need to realize that Jesus demands that we trust Him as Lord over all our lives or He will not be Lord of our lives at all. Jesus has too much to offer to be forced to settle into second place.

The Lord has given me permission, in this book, to say that if we will not trust Him totally and completely, then He reserves the right and He has the power to find some new people who will wholeheartedly surrender to Him. When this happens, those who have forsaken and rejected Him are then left to fight the devil and try to figure out life all by themselves. I believe this is the reason Jesus goes to such great lengths to reveal *His personality* to us, expose *His power* before us, and manifest *His presence* through us.

HE IS MORE THAN ABLE

It is through the I AM statements of Jesus that we discover what kind of Savior we are trusting in and the multiplicity of His abilities. If you are in a relationship with Jesus, you are linked with a Savior who does not submit to any other superior, He does not answer to any other authority, and He does not report to any other ruler. The omnipotence of Jesus gives Him full freedom, so no circumstance can restrict Him, no adversity can hinder Him, no situation can constrain Him, no enemy can defeat Him, and no obstacle can block Him! He is the great I AM. He is not the I was, He is not the I will be. He is the great I AM.

Allow me to take a moment to call the roll and let you know all that is a part of the I AM statements of Jesus.

He is the I AM who gives us spiritual bread to nourish our hungry and starving souls.

He is the I AM who brings the luminous, refulgent light to the darkest areas of our lives.

He is the I AM who grants us entrance into a relationship with Himself as the doorway of salvation.

He is the I AM who leads us every day of our lives as the Good Shepherd.

He is the I AM who gives us hope for new life when we find ourselves in the midst of some dead and dying situations. He reminds us that He is the resurrection and the life.

> *He is the I AM who is the way out of sin, the*
> *truth about who God is, and the life that will*
> *outlast time and every pain we experience on*
> *this side of the grave.*

With all of that in mind, we now come to
what most skilled commentators call the final
I AM statement of Jesus, which is a part of the
Upper Room Discourse. The Passover feast
had been celebrated. The Lord's Supper had
been instituted. The bread had been eaten.
The wine had been consumed. The feet of the
disciples had been washed. The betrayer had
been exposed and Judas had already left the
table. Jesus was working with the eleven men
who were left.

LET THEM GO

Before we move any further, I want you to
notice what Jesus *did not* do. He *did not* waste
any time talking about the plot Judas had set
for Him. He did not waste any time asking
why Judas would betray Him after all He had
done for him. Judas "went out immediately"
(John 13:30). And Jesus let him go. I think

this is a lesson we all need to learn. When people get ready to leave our lives, we need to learn how to let them go and get back to focusing on what the Lord has commanded us to do. This is exactly what Jesus did.

JESUS'S MENTAL AND PHYSICAL PREPARATION BEFORE HIS DEATH

Jesus's focus at the Last Supper was on doing two basic things.

- First, He was preparing Himself mentally for Calvary. Jesus knew He was getting ready to die in a public and very humiliating fashion. He also knew He was going to leave these men physically in just a few days—after His ascension from the grave.

- Secondly, He was preparing His disciples for the massive and enormous work that lay ahead of them: the work of teaching, preaching, evangelizing, and spreading the gospel throughout the entire world. This was an assignment that was going to begin

just fifty short days after His
resurrection.

These men did not know the enormity of
the situation waiting for them, but Jesus did,
so He was careful and painstakingly precise in
His communication with them. The Master
knew every spiritual "I" needed to be dotted
and every divine "T" needed to be crossed.

We hear Jesus as He spoke these words. "I
am the true vine, and My Father is the
vinedresser. Every branch in Me that does not
bear fruit He takes away; and every branch
that bears fruit He prunes, that it may bear
more fruit" (John 15:1–2).

PERFECTLY POSTURED FOR PRODUCTIVITY

If we are going to take full advantage of the
fact that we have been *perfectly postured for
productivity,* the first thing we need to focus
on is what I want to call:

I: THE REVELATION OF HIS PURITY

Jesus said, "I am the true vine" (v.15). This
word "true" seems to imply there were other
vines that were false, and false vines only

produce false fruit. We need to know that the world has vines known as earthly vines. They depend on this world's system to provide for and meet their needs. This helped me to understand that we need to be careful about whom we allow ourselves to become connected to.

The truth of the matter is: whomever we connect with has the power to produce in us a replica of him/herself. Just as connecting with Jesus produces Christians, connecting with worldly demons produces other little worldly devils! Jesus was trying to get us to understand that when we remain connected to Him, our lives will produce holy and righteous fruit.

We will produce some merciful melons of music, some wonderful wheat of the Word, some powerful plums of praise, and some godly grapes of grace. But when we allow ourselves to get hooked up with the wrong people and become attached to the wrong vines, we will then start to produce some bad fruit: things like the afflicted apples of arrogance, bad bananas of bitterness, lying lemons of laziness, rotten raisins of resentment, and grungy grapefruits of gossip. This leads me to ask what kind of fruit is coming out of your life., because whatever you are connected to is what you will produce. Jesus wanted these disciples, and He wants us, to know He was connected to God, and only godly things could be produced in His life.

The question may be raised that if we are children of God and if we have truly been connected to Jesus, then why is it that we have so much bad fruit in our lives? The answer is relatively simple. It is because we have been giving too many other people "planting privileges." We allow them to plant anger in our hearts, doubt in our minds, resentment in our souls, and bitterness in our spirits. As a result, we are all torn and twisted on the inside. We have the good seed from Jesus along with other bad seed received from negative people. We need to learn how to tell people we are not going to allow them to pollute our minds with all of that negative mess. That is why the verse goes on to say, "My Father is the vinedresser" (v.1).

This word "vinedresser" refers to the gardener of vines, the horticulturist of the vineyard. My Father is the one who makes sure every weed of adversity is pulled up out of Me before it ever has a chance to take root and grow in my life. It also means My Father is the one who protects me and makes sure the enemy cannot come in and contaminate me. People said negative things to Jesus, but He did not allow those things to grow in His heart. I have discovered that when we allow people to fill us with bad seed, it will affect our sleep, our jobs, and our witness and have a bad effect on our relationships. Those same people who cause the trouble will be doing just fine while we are nervous wrecks, all because we are allowing them to use us to carry their bad baggage around. Jesus wants us to know that He is the true vine, and His Father made sure that His life remained pure. He wants to do the same thing for each and every one of us.

But then, secondly, verse 2 reads like this, "Every branch in Me that does not bear fruit

He takes away." And that leads us to our second point of emphasis which I want to call:

II: THE READJUSTMENT OF OUR POSITION

When Jesus made this statement, it almost appears as though He was saying we can be connected to Him at one moment and then disconnected from Him the next moment. But all of us know this is not possible because of the doctrine called eternal security. "I give them eternal life, and they shall never perish; neither shall anyone snatch them out of My hand" (John 10:28). Since the Lord will not allow anyone else to snatch us out of His hand, then surely He will not cut us off from Himself once we have become a part of Him.

The question then needs to be answered, what did Jesus mean when He said, "Every branch in Me that does not bear fruit He takes away"? The answer is found in the proper and correct interpretation of the phrase "takes away." This does not mean to remove, cut off, or disconnect; it means to lift, to elevate, or to raise. This phrase "takes away," in its original

Greek entomology, means the same as our English word for airplane.

If the vinedressers in Jerusalem had branches in the field that were not producing grapes, they would not cut them off; they would go into the field and prop them up with small wooden sticks so they could be exposed to more sunlight. The problem with their being unfruitful was that they were living too low—they were comfortable in the shade and they were not getting enough sun. There it is! Jesus is saying that whenever we are not producing any fruit for the kingdom of God, it is because we are living too low. We have become comfortable in the shade of our hideout areas and we are not getting close enough to the sunlight of God's Word. He has to lift us up, take us away from the ground of our comfort zone, and force us to live in the hot sun of His exposure. Many of us have become comfortable hiding out in the shade of nonproductivity, so the Lord will readjust our position in order to get a greater level of productiveness from us.

If it seems like things are beginning to heat up in your life and you are starting to feel like you are moving out of your comfort zone, it is all because the Lord knows you have been hiding out in the sinful shade long enough. It is now time for you to be raised to a new level of living. Did you not know that the only reason the Lord is allowing things to warm up in your life is because He knows His divine heat has a way of producing a new level of godly holiness within you?

Not only does the Lord make the facts clear to us that we have been *perfectly postured for productivity* so we might see the *revelation of his purity,* and experience the readjustment of our positions, but we also need what I want to call:

III: THE REMOVAL OF THE POISON

Now, just in case you may be wondering where this is coming from, it is right here in the text. In verse 2, Jesus went on to say, "And every branch that bears fruit He prunes." This word "prunes" (or purges) means to clean and remove the negative stuff from the branch without destroying the branch itself. This helped me to realize that while some of us are saved and we are a connected part of the body of Christ, our problem lies in the fact that we are still connected to some ungodly things.

There will be times in our lives when Jesus will purposefully cut and clean people and possessions from us to get a greater level of productivity out of us. When I look back over my own life, I can see how the Lord has caused this process to move our church to where it is today. In 2004, the Lord purged some people out of our church and we bought seven acres of land. In 2006, He purged some other people and we built a one-million-dollar sanctuary. In 2007, He purged some more people and we built our fellowship hall. In 2009, we went through another purging and I wrote my first book, *A Marvelous Model of Ministry.* Then in 2011, we went through another purging and we built our $700,000 family life center.

To date I have completed two additional books prior to this one, *Making a Difference in the Kingdom of God* and *365 Days of*

Devotion, Development, and Discipline with Jesus. I've received invitations to preach in more revivals in six months than I was previously preaching in two years. We have seen our offerings increase, started a live streaming video ministry, strengthened our church school ministry, added new disciples to our men's ministry, and started a Wisdom Speaks women's ministry. In addition, we serve our community through Meals on Wheels and Garments & Groceries from Grace, which serve more families than ever before. We give thousands of dollars in scholarship money each year. It appears the purging process is working to me. That is why we should not always cry and get sad when some people and some possessions leave our lives. It just may be that God is getting ready to bring us to a greater level of spiritual success. The Lord knows there may be some relationships that need to be purged. There are some outside responsibilities that need to be purged, and there are some restraints that need to be purged. I need to be honest and tell you the purging process is a painful process, but it is also a productive process.

Jesus said the purpose behind it all is for us to "bear more fruit" (v.2).

I have asked us to examine the *revelation of his purity, the readjustment of our positions,* and *the removal of the poison,* but finally, let me say a word about:

IV: The Release of our Productivity

Jesus wants us to know that after the purging process is complete, we should be ready not just to bear fruit, but to "bear more fruit" (v.2). In other words, when the Lord has removed those negative things and people from our lives, we should be ready to do at least three things.

1) Let everybody know who we are *connected* to.
2) Let everybody know who we are *committed* to.
3) Let everybody know who our *celebration* is offered to.

You may be feeling as if no one knows what you are going through but the Lord. You just may be absolutely correct about that. But as a child of God, in the midst of an absence of seeming humanistic empathy, you have the greatest power and presence still active and available to you. His name is Jesus Christ. Be encouraged.

He is all you or I will ever need!

ABOUT THE AUTHOR

Reverend Brackins is a native of Houston, TX, and a preaching son of the True Light Baptist Church of Houston. He serves as President Emeritus of the board of directors for One Church One Child, Inc. and as the assistant treasurer for the Black Ecumenical Leadership Alliance. He is a member of the National Baptist Convention of America International, Inc., where he has served and worked with the evangelical board for more than thirty years.

Reverend Brackins is the founding pastor of the Grace Tabernacle Baptist Church which had her genesis in 1987. The church has grown from twenty-seven members with two ministries to better than 400 active members, with more than twenty-five vibrant, need-meeting ministries since her beginning. The church offers an outreach center called Garments and Groceries from Grace. This outreach center opened in 2002 and is tailored exclusively to meet the needs of those in the community of the Grace Tabernacle Church who are less fortunate.

In 2014, Pastor Brackins was recognized for his outstanding service in the Christian community by the St. Thomas Christian University of Jacksonville, Florida, with an honorary Doctor of Divinity degree. Pastor Brackins is also a musician: he plays the guitar, bass, piano, and organ. He has preached extensively throughout much of America, and his greatest passion is the preaching of the gospel to the end that lost souls are won to Jesus Christ.

Roy is married to Pamela Doreen Brackins. They are the proud parents of four children.

If you would like to contact Dr Brackins:
Website: www.gracetabernaclechurch.org
E-mail: gtabernacl@aol.com

OTHER BOOKS BY THE AUTHOR

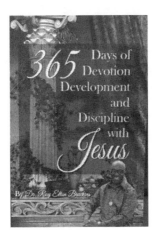

365 DAYS OF DEVOTION, DEVELOPMENT, & DISCIPLINE WITH JESUS

Most daily devotionals include only words of inspiration and encouragement, but through this labor of love, the Lord provides the opportunity for us to grow in at least three dimensions of our relationship with him. Many helpful hints are provided on how to enhance our devotion with the Lord, our development in the Lord, and our disciplines to become more like the Lord.

MAKING A DIFFERENCE IN THE KINGDOM OF GOD

Dr Roy Elton Brackins helps those of us in the body of Christ maximize our God-given potential in three very important areas. Our surrender to the Word of God, our service in the work of God, and our stewardship of the wealth of God. This book is extremely practical and a great tool for developing our relationship with Jesus Christ and our representation of Him.

A MARVELOUS MODEL OF MINISTRY

We live in a time when many of us feel that the ability to fulfill God's purpose for our lives is inextricably tied to our having a massive amount of money and other resources to work with. Yet God is still looking for people who will serve as "men in the middle," those who will make the best of what they have been given by God.

Made in the USA
Middletown, DE
03 April 2021